The Unpainted South

McCrea pack house, Central, S.C.

THE UNPAINTED SOUTH

CAROLINA'S VANISHING WORLD

PHOTOGRAPHS *by* Selden B. Hill   SONGS *and* POEMS *by* William P. Baldwin

EVENING POST PUBLISHING COMPANY
Charleston
South Carolina

EVENINGPOSTBOOKS
Our Accent is Southern!
www.EveningPostBooks.com

Published by
Evening Post Books
Charleston, South Carolina
www.EveningPostBooks.com

Photographs Copyright © 2011 Selden B. Hill; Text Copyright © William P. Baldwin
Editor: John M. Burbage
Designer: Carley Wilson Brown

Front cover photo: Wilson, South Carolina
Photo of Selden B. Hill by Wade Spees; Photo of William P. Baldwin by John McWilliams

"Pure history," Henry, S.C.

Second Edition, December 2011
Printed and bound in the USA by Sun Printing

A CIP catalog record for this book has been applied for from the Library of Congress.

ISBN: 978-0-9834457-1-5

Dry pump, Salters, S.C.

Pineville Chapel, Pineville, S.C.

V

ACKNOWLEDGEMENTS

Our creative director and designer, Carley Wilson Brown, did more than cut and paste. She lent her country-bred spirit to this book. Thank you, Carley.

And Mindy Burgin edited lyrics, set songs to music, and best of all kept me honest. Thank you, Mindy.

For moral support and advice I'd like to thank Sam Savage, Harlan Greene, David Hane, Alex Moore, Dale Rosengarten, Stephanie Waldron, John McWilliams, MaryLou Thomson, Melanie Hartnett, Maria Kirby-Smith, Lynda Solansky, Ellen Solomon, Richard Wyndham, Sherry Browne, Susan Hindman, Anne Knight and Sam Watson, Alice Jordan, Patty and Jim Fulcher, V. Elizabeth Turk, Pete and Claudia Kornack, Aida Rogers, Dan Lesesne, Bill McCullough, Karen Shuler and my favorite librarians Pat Gross and Janice Knight. For religious instruction and great friendship Rev. Jennie Olbrych, Rev. Callie Perkins, Rev. Dick Thomson and Dr. Walter Cook. Darcy Shankland at *Charleston Magazine* got me started in the country music business. Thanks to Robert Epps for sharing his amazing country music collection and to Rut Leland for musical insights. For final proofing, Jamie Pohlman. For keeping the computer going and their usual patience, my sons, Aaron and Malcolm Baldwin and my old friend Gary Bronson. For everything my wife, Lil.

Those familiar with 19th century poetry will quickly spot the influence of Emily Dickinson, Rudyard Kipling and Christina Rossetti. I was ruthless in borrowing from these. But I make no apologies. They are dead and gone and should be beyond such concerns. The same goes for the 17th century poet John Donne. And I played fast and loose with Shakespeare. Wordsworth, too. Actually, anyone my long-suffering Clemson professors exposed me to was considered fair game. I also borrowed from my friends. The poem *Margarite* is based closely on Alice Jordan's memoir *Margarite*. *Brother*, *Main Street* and *A Passing* all grew out of conversations with Carley

Train depot loading ramp, Conway, S.C.

Brown. *Alcolu*, *Lone Star* and several others suggest the photographing experiences of Bud Hill. If a poem or song is named with a reference to a particular person then it's likely that person influenced the writing in a direct way. The process of composition depended a great deal on feedback (often over the internet) from those listed in the first of the acknowledgement. I am in particular debt to Sam Savage and Harlan Greene for their assistance with this process.

Thank you to Katelin McGory and Holly Holladay of Evening Post Books. To Katelin for her sales and marketing expertise and to Holly for her help in the editing process. A special thanks to John Burbage of Evening Post Publishing for his continuing support. And last but not least, thanks to Dr. Eddie White and Nat Mundy of Awendaw Green for their indispensible help in completing the CD version of *The Unpainted South*.

—WB

Thank you Erin Browne for taking the time to order my second, not so cheap, really good camera. And I have to thank you and your adorable little daughter, Isi, for listening and for encouraging.

Thanks to the many understanding people of the Lowcountry that share my belief that America's landscape is changing much too rapidly. Thank you all for welcoming me to your farms and properties and for allowing me to roam them at will. The wonderful history you shared gave me a better understanding of your community and of the people who lived and labored there. The images that I focused on were influenced by the stories you told. You all brought your properties to life for me. Among those who were so free with their land and lore are: George Cooper, Swinton Ward and his daughter, David McCrea, Dan Daniels (a man so interesting they named him the same thing twice), David McKenzie and the charming and gracious Dr. Heather Shuler, whom I met on New Year's morning 2011. I especially enjoyed meeting Dr. Shuler, as any woman who shares my love for an old A-framed chicken coop is someone very special.

To Gay and Joel Horry who opened their Gillisonville home to us: Thanks for the hospitality, the good conversation and the wonderful food. Touring the lower part of the state was made much easier by your generosity.

A special thank you goes to my friends in McClellanville who shared their Pinckney Street Kitchen lunch breaks with me and reviewed the photos taken on my ramblings. Patty Fulcher and Richard Wyndham patiently looked through the stack of prints and always found at least one to praise. Elizabeth Turk reviewed them all, hundreds and hundreds of photos, and spent hours educating and encouraging . . . thank you, too. And thanks to Russell Tyler for encouragement and advice and those directions to places that didn't exist.

Thanks to the members and volunteers of The Village Museum for allowing me to take so much time away from my favorite project of all. Nothing means more to me than the preservation of the history and culture of "the Village."

To my sisters Becky and Susan and to my brother Henry, thank you for believing in my talent for all these many, many years.

And lastly, thank you, my cousin and dear friend Billy Baldwin for encouraging me to believe that all the time spent traveling the back roads of the Lowcounty was worthwhile and for reassuring me time and time again that the beauty I find in a rusty-roofed tobacco barn or falling-down farmhouse will not go unnoticed or unappreciated.

—SH

Farmyard gate, Carvers Bay, S.C.

PROLOGUE

The Unpainted South is an ambitious book, for with mere photographs and words we wished to say, "Take a look. Here's the South." At least here are the remnants. The South we knew as boys and as young men is gone—and for the better. The miserable legacy of racism and poverty is gradually lessening. Living conditions, salaries and civil rights, health care and education have all improved. Indoor plumbing, electricity and super highways: these days they're taken for granted. But hasn't that been done at the cost of romance, mystery, eccentricity—all that made the poetic South? It's not our intent to argue this was a poor swap. It wasn't. Making omelets requires the breaking of eggs. Not that you can buy eggs within McClellanville's town limits. A village of 450 and as of last week to sell an egg your chicken lays requires a health inspection and a business license. Oh, the world is too much with us.

Tar paper shredded by storms, Andrews, S.C.

Now, it's not like one day Selden "Bud" Hill picked up a camera and set off with the intention of photographing every collapsing barn between the Savannah River and the North Carolina border and inland to Interstate 95. Well, actually he did do that, but there's more. After a year of photographing he decided the camera was too cheap, bought a better one and took every photograph over, then a year later got a polarizing lense and did half of them for a third time. For three years and for roughly three days a week, Bud set out in his Ford F-150 at dawn, drove those secondary roads, the farm-to-market highways we were once so proud of, and recorded the passing of the old-time farming way of life. Of course, much of the land is still farmed. Fly over South Carolina or any other Southern state and you look down on an amazing patchwork of fields under cultivation. But the small family farm is a thing of the past. And on both sides of the highway, you will find frame houses and barns in a state of collapse, fields gone to broom sedge and pine trees. A similar fate has come to the small country towns. Main streets and even residential areas are abandoned, sometimes completely. Churches and schools are boarded up. The rural South today is Bud's subject matter.

I came to the project two years after Bud began. I'd been looking at his photographs on a weekly basis when one particular group inspired me to write the song *Country for Sale*. The contrast between the country Bud was photographing and what was being celebrated by today's rock and roll country performers seemed vast indeed. Not surprisingly the song was a good match to Bud's effort, so we decided to collaborate on a book. At about the same time I teamed up with the organist in my church, Mindy Burgin, who began to write music and record the songs that followed. And soon afterward I began to write the poetry you'll also find in these pages.

Bud says he photographs in Walker Evans' style, and as I was a big fan of Evans' collaborator, James Agee, I'm tempted to go along. But in fact, Bud brings more affection and slightly less irony to his work than Evans did. Mid-Westerner Wright Morris is a better fit. When asked about the difference between Morris and Evans, Morris replied something to the effect, "We both photograph a chair, but I love that chair." I say the same for Bud Hill. He loves these collapsing tobacco barns and every country store and country church he comes across.

Still, if we're looking for a precedent, I'm going out on a limb and offering Clarence John Laughlin's catalogue of deserted plantation houses, *Ghosts Along the Mississippi*. As a part of the greater whole, Bud and I have touched briefly on the Plantation South, but I think we share Laughlin's "poetical vision." The South is more than the sum total of a photograph and an accompanying poem. The South is indescribable, a mystical experience. Our intention is to simply point you in the right direction.

Before closing, I should mention the strong religious content of *The Unpainted South*. Bud's a great and constant photographer of churches and accompanying graveyards. I'm a devout, if slightly skewed, Episcopalian, and at the least provocation will write a poem or song to my notion of Godly specifications. As this was a Christ-specifying landscape, that proved to be a timely fit.

And now I'll leave you with the closing words of Clarence John Laughlin: "This then is the South . . . from which, clutched by the hand of memory, something of a deathless magic eludes the blows of time."

— *William Baldwin*
McClellanville, South Carolina　　　　Summer 2011

Ice cream for sale, near Claussen, S.C.

Something to think about, Andrews, S.C.

COUNTRY FOR SALE
DeSoto on blocks
This song is for you
Live bait, live bait,
I'm singing you too.
Oceans are rising
Banks going fail
Look around, Mister,
Country's for sale.

Jesus is coming.
Gourds hanging high,
Front pew music
The sweet bye and bye.
World's in collision,
Check's in the mail
Look around, Sister,
Country's for sale.

Mailbox, mailbox,
A bright bottle tree,
Deer crossing here
And the air's still free.
But life wants to gallop
And it's ride, Devil, ride.
Listen up, Brother,
Country's lost pride.

Tobacco Barn memory
When morning means five,
One Goody Powder
Will keep you alive.
But the cows in the corn
The radio's on
Listen there, Sister,
Country's long gone.

Oh, radio, radio,
Television too.
Modern-day country
I'm pointing at you.
World's in collision,
Dog lost the trail.
Look around, Sister,
Country's for sale.

DeSoto on blocks
This song is for you
Live bait, live bait,
I'm singing you too.
Oceans are rising
Dikes going fail
Look around, Mister,
Country's for sale.

This former neighborhood store and Bible study building is now without customers or students. Cainhoy, S.C.

Classic white picket fence, Claussen House, Claussen, S.C.

THOUGHTS

Just to hear *Take courage* has you longing
For a simpler time.
And *Be of good cheer* you won't find that
Except on greeting cards.
Where'd they go,
Those antique sympathies?
Cheap sentiments. We've got them by the score.
What we need is more quaint encouragements.
Thoughts dearly bought
By trials and desperate measures,
And Love undivided, unrefined.

Gateway to farm, Shulerville, S.C.

13

Livestock barn and cornfield, Green Sea, S.C.

Seems like such a waste
Fifty years
And who will know
This thorny land
Where with his Love
And one small
Sign, Jesus comes
To save us all.
from "Jesus Saves with One Small Sign"

Contradiction in Suttons, S.C.

Impressive gravestone, Shulerville, S.C.

JESUS SAVES WITH ONE SMALL SIGN

Seems like such a waste
Fifty years
And who will know
This thorny land
Where with his Love
And one small
Sign, Jesus comes
To save us all.

Hard hands a cradle
For her breasts.
By God's grace
With children they are blessed.

Mountains dim and oceans fade.
Child begotten, crop unmade.
Job in town but he's
Not paid.
She says:
You don't listen to me
Do you?
He says:
I'm listening now.
And then she smiles

The strife and toil
Enacted here
Upon this soil
A living in the good years
And none at all the rest.
How did a couple do this?
Go on, if you know
Confess.
He says:
I never promised
Riches.
She says:
We'll spend them
Sparkling stars.

COUNTRY CEMETERY

These settled ones
Are quiet dust,
Unless we've had a rain.
Then puddles form where
Hearts once beat
And tears have matted pain.

POEM FOR MY WIFE

A dirt road led towards the pines
Beside a battered field.
The harvester had come this way
And left a scattered meal.

A doe, in quiet, stepped
Into the fading light
As stars, in ordination,
Eased into the night.

Road through a cornfield, Andrews, S.C.

Farmhouse missing siding, Lone Star, S.C.

EDEN WAS THAT FARMHOUSE
Eden was that farmhouse
We slept in every night.
We didn't have a clue
Thought Eden ours by right.

You washed your hands?
Biscuits, grits and ham.
You got your school?
Granny cries, Oh, lands.

Oh, lands! The bus! The bus!
The bus! The bus!
It waited then.
I want it now to wait for us.

Put Papa in the barn again
The black dog in the sun.
The cat can be in Mama's arms.
And here I'll come,
With school books
All a-tumbling.

How strange to be
Off running. To catch
A yellow bus. And trust
That house will wait for us.

Eden was that big oak tree
We climbed near out of sight
We didn't have a clue
Thought Eden ours by right

Who's that up there with you?
Boy come down. Don't make
Me call your daddy, now.
Granny cries, Land sake.

Sally with the raven hair.
That's you, girl, you up there?
Don't give us such a scare.
Boy, get that girl down here.
And down here we come
All a-tumbling.

Oh, how strange
To be off running
To claim a
Promised kiss, and trust

That tree will wait for us.
That tree will wait for us.

Leafless now,
There it stands,
That oak is coming down
They're clearing ground.
To make a clearing,
Don't ask me why.
Sally went from here
And so, of course, did I.

How odd on looking back.
Us charging 'round this place
We didn't have a clue
Our Eden'd be misplaced.

How odd on looking back.
Me charging from the place
Why couldn't I have sensed
Our Eden'd be misplaced?

Crack cocaine bringing pain
Broken children here, there.
Where's the care?
Children lost to
God knows what
We had this Eden all around
And didn't know to fear.
Had Paradise beneath our feet
And didn't know
Just how sweet
It was.

Cornfield in pine woods with watering tub, Carvers Bay, S.C.

Plymouth collecting dust in tobacco barn, Millwood Community, S.C.

Gap in decorative wrought iron fence, St. Matthews, S.C.

CONQUERING HEROES

A yellow dog defends the porch
Speckled guineas charging.
Half-past five I think it was
Four o'clock was blooming.

He says
Now, you don't know me do you?
I've been from here awhile.
I used to come and stand right there
Just to watch you smile.

She says,
I raised three kids for Mama
While you were off at war
Fought losing battles every day.
I'm ready to withdraw.

He says,
Well, I think I got your meaning
I watched buddies fall
Fought losing battles every day
Until I heard your call.

She says,
I did not know you'd heard me.
I stood here in the yard.
And whispered to the night wind
Bring him home unharmed.

And
With that they both surrendered.
Flew white flags all around.
The yellow dog hushed himself.
The guineas gave up ground.
'Cause love's the greatest conqueror:
They claim it conquers all.

Double side porches and staircase, Elloree, S.C.

Shingle and brick turret, Branchville, S.C.

Turret with high pitched roof, Andrews, S.C.

Architectural details across the Lowcountry.

Old barn sits back from the road framed by trees and bushes, Hebron, S.C.

BUD'S SONG

If flowers came uprooted
And chased after bees
If boats were on land
And churches out to sea.
If ponies rode on men
And not the other way around
I'd know I'd lost her love,
'Cause the world'd be upside down.

If money grew on trees,
And apples came from Congress
If babies knew their fathers
And GE gave us progress,
If laws just served the men
And not the other way around,
I'd know I'd lost all reason,
'Cause the world'd be upside down.

If life was but a mirror
And death no other side,
If Gabe gave up his crawfish
And Ford trucks lost their ride.
If all these things had happened
And not the other way around,
I'd say goodbye to friendships,
'Cause the world'd be upside down.

Pecan tree and mailbox, Vance, S.C.

25

Barn surrounded by young trees, Eutawville, S.C.

Log barn and oak tree, Trio, S.C.

House with zig-zag drainpipe in cotton field, Choppee, S.C.

Tree art, Choppee, S.C.

Hanging gourd, Cubbedge Hill, S.C.

Little garden girl, Robertville, S.C.

McCrea's stable and pack house, Central, S.C.

The Proposal

Brought over from the county seat.
It was a race horse that she beat.
To the road's end and back again.
Barefoot she ran
With skirt bunched up in her hand.
People clapping, dogs a-yapping.
That's how she won her man,
And their son had a son.
Who had a son. He's that one.
Not so fleet of foot.
Not so sure of right.
Not so fond of risk.
But if I'd spend the night,
He'd take a turn around the track.
He'd drive his truck down there and back.

First woman graduate of our school
To kill a grown man in a duel.
He said this ain't a woman's part.
She said it is
Then shot him straight through the heart.
People clapping, dogs a-yapping
That's how she saved her man.
And their son had a son.
Who had a son. He's that one.

Corn stored in derelict cabin, Suttons, S.C.

Scarecrow in a melon patch, Jordanville, S.C.

Not so fleet of foot.
Not so sure of right.
Not so fond of risk.
But if I'd spend the night,
He'd take a turn around the track.
He'd drive his truck down there and back.

She was last of all the family
To never try and tell a lie.
She stood here. He stood there.
To take their vows
On fifty Bibles, this she swore:
I'll never ever do you wrong.
He loved her ever more
And their son had a son.
Who had a son. He's that one.
Not so fleet of foot.
Not so sure of right.
Not so fond of risk.
But if I'd spend the night,
He'd take a turn around the track.
He'd drive his truck down there and back.

Leaning storage shed, McClellanville, S.C.

Abandoned home in field, Pleasant Hill, S.C.

A house that goes unpainted
For a man that doesn't care.
It's well beyond the roadside
A place to step with care.
Got the mattress in the kitchen,
The porch is pulled away,
The roof is losing shingles,
The windows dirty gray.
He's lost the will to paint that house
And the need to love her too,
But she's coming by tomorrow
And she claims she'll pull them through.
from "Sans Paint"

View from porch, Suttons, S.C.

Light through doorway, Cooper Academy, Lake City, S.C.

ANOTHER HOPE
Another hope of mine
Dying on the vine,
Lost among the rotten melon rinds
And those ripe red tomatoes
That went yellow-belly up.
Don't ask me how my garden grows.
The earthly delights are a disaster,
Even worse than last year
When the blight
Carried off your smile.

Gourd and birdhouse tree, Center, S.C.

Drying clothes on the back porch, Aynor, S.C.

Kudzu and bamboo surround building at railroad crossing, Creston, S.C.

Silhouette of bridge perfectly frames water view of Sammy Swamp, near Paxville, S.C.

Small boats seem suspended between fog and water, Jeremy Creek, McClellanville, S.C.

BLUFFTON

Hiding and seek.
Two, three, four, five...
Coming ready or not,
God's blessings arise.
Dogs are determined,
We children are too.
Lightning bugs dancing,
Summer's near through.
You can live out a memory.
I know that that's true.
Hiding and seek.
What else do we do?

Rope swing over swimming hole on the Black River, near Andrews, S.C.

Granny Magwood's bateau tied up at Jeremy Creek, McClellanville, S.C.

CAPTAIN DICKINSON'S SONG
Useless the winds
To a heart in port—
Done with the compass,
Done with the chart.
Rowing in Eden!
Oh! The sea!
Honey come rowing
Tonight with me.

Just two good oars
And the stars for free.
Has there ever been
Such a luxury?
Rowing in Eden!
Oh! The sea!
Honey come rowing
Tonight with me

Oceans get lonely
Where lands they meet.
A touch from waves
Then waves retreat.
Rowing in Eden!
Oh! The sea!
Honey come rowing
Tonight with me

People are lonely
They chance to meet.
A touch from his hand
No. Don't you retreat
Just look at that surf
Tossing free
Honey, come along
Anchor with me.

Dock at sunset, the Intercostal Waterway at Cape Romain, S.C.

Episcopal Chapel of Ease, McClellanville, S.C.

A SONG FOR SISTER PETERKIN

Heaven is a beautiful place
A place of Dogs and Flowers
And all of those who get there
Are granted special powers.

We'll touch the beating hearts
Of family, friends and lovers.
We'll skip along on streets of gold
And dream beneath cloud covers.

We'll listen to God's music
With ears that hear no blame
And when we sing his praises
It'll be with tongues of flame.

Clarendon Baptist Church, Alcolu, S.C.

Catholic Hill Church, Catholic Hill, S.C.

A LITTLE CHURCH IS BETTER

A little church is better
Than two big ones.
Especially when the road's
No wider than this run.
Doesn't take but three good
Voices to get a choir brewing.
Songs bounce off the rafters
And all of them are fine ones.
Doesn't take but three true
Hearts to get His Love across.
Praise comes out the windows.
Go on and bring a crew in.

Small rural churches, Oakridge Community, Hardeeville, Cross, and Jacksonboro, S.C.

The "old brick church," Salem Black River Church, Mayesville, S.C.

Entrance to Presbyterian churchyard and graveyard, Indiantown, S.C.

Graveyard gate, Salem Black River Church, Mayesville, S.C.

View from the old church towards the new,
near Huger, S.C.

WEDDING DAY

Moon goes down.
Sun won't rise.
Black, black clouds.
Wedding day sighs.
Love's for losers.
And losers pay.
Caterer cussing
And priest lost his way.

Husband to be
I got three things to say:
I love you,
I love you
And maybe
I do.

Wedding cake
Some mistake
Broke in half
'Cause just half-baked.
Maid of honor
Claims she's all through
Can't zip that mess
And there's two left shoes.

Best man's drunk
Lost the ring.
Solo singer
Claims she can't sing.
She wants silence
And all the while.
His ex-wife's laughing.
Dog's in the aisle.

Husband to be
I got three things to say,
I love you,
I love you
And maybe I do.

When we met,
I knew then
Here's a man
Can be my friend.
He thinks the same,
Wants a friend for life,
Says tell me, honey,
Will you be my wife?

And now it's over,
We're man and wife
I do and I did and this one is for life.

Robertville Baptist Church, Robertville, S.C.

City of Myrtle Beach passenger train, circa 1957, Conway, S.C.

Fog and reflection, railroad trestle at Jamestown, S.C.

Chinaberry trees obscure the view of the old train depot, Cades, S.C.

LOVE SONG

He came from a far-off planet
Traveled down the Seaboard line.
He said, Honey, you're wasted in this place.
You'll just wither away on the vine.

Now the promise that he made, it wasn't to her.
Nor did he care what her mama must bear.
He took apart her country-bred heart
And threw away six pieces.

One piece fed the east wind.
Two pieces went to the west.
The other three were reckless spent
By that near to a perfect fool,
Who claimed he knew what was best.

No windows. No walls. No face she recalls.
Just his voice on the telephone line.
He said, Honey, you're wasted in that place.
You'll wither away on the vine.

And he plucked her down to a place
That she found.
Wasn't nearly so fine.
Wasn't nearly so fine.
A place that wasn't
Nearly so fine.

Passenger car and flowering weeds, Kingstree, S.C.

Former U.S. Post Office leans slightly, Lane, S.C.

Oak limbs hang above post office, Pinopolis, S.C.

Boarded and abandoned, post office at Fort Motte, S.C.

Back door of thrift store and post office building, Sardinia, S.C.

FEED STORE ROMANCE

Corn silk curls and cherry lips.
She went traipsing down the aisle,
I raised my hat a notch or two
And risked a little smile.
Then went about my business,
Like I knew what post holes were.
Traced those happy boot steps,
And kept on watching her.

I met her at the feed store.
What more for me to say?
I fell in love 'tween worming dogs
And that mash that makes hens lay.
Oh, I know some day I'll find her.
I know that day will come.
I know she needs a farmer.
And I'm bound to be the one.

She took her own sweet time.
She'd be so fine to kiss
Way she read at all those labels,
And studied on her list.
Mam, oh mam,
Can I help with that?
Can I take it to your truck?
A hundred pounds of chicken scratch.
I've often toted such.

The incubator? Pile it on.
That mule collar too.
Rock salt? In my left hand.
What else can I do for you?
A name? Oh yeah.
I got a name.
It's kind of you to ask.
Same name as my daddy,
Honey, watch the door.
You're traveling mighty fast.

D. P. Cooper's Country Store at Cooper's Crossing, near Salters, S.C.

Purina Check-R-Mix Store, Branchville, S.C.

I loaded up the truck
Well, yeah, I'm kind of sweet.
Tote things just for pretty girls?
How else we going to meet?
Then my smiling lips she kissed.
And drove away real quick.
She'd charged it all to me.
Cops say she's pretty slick.
I say she's pretty pretty.
She never said her name.
I know that I been blistered,
And love her all the same.
What? You don't mean it.

I just think the girl is bold.
Save that pity that you're feeling
For the guy whose truck she stole.

I met her at the feed store.
What more for me to say?
I fell in love 'tween worming dogs
And that mash that makes hens lay.
Oh, I know some day I'll find her.
I know that day will come.
I know she needs a farmer.
And I'm bound to be the one.

Sign of the past, Henry, S.C.

Neighborhood convenience stores have replaced old-fashioned country stores, Mullins, S.C.

Yesterday's advertisements, Santee and Carvers Bay, S.C.

Texaco gas station at Christmas time, Green Pond, S.C.

Swinton Ward looks thoughtfully out across his store, Ward's Grocery Store, Trio, S.C.

The Speckled Bird: Ward's Grocery

My daddy painted houses.
My daddy played with words.
My daddy drove an old pickup
He called the Speckled Bird.

Every house he'd painted
He dripped some on that truck,
A seventy-two Ford half-ton,
His speckled bird pickup.

Scraping paint then priming
Forty hours a week and more.
Boy, tell me what you do today?
Him coming through the door.

Nothing, Daddy, nothing.
Well, go on and get your cuz.
(Next house over was my cousin.
A best friend that cousin was.)

We're riding in the Speckled Bird
And it's out to Ward's Grocery.
He'd get a cold beer for himself
 And Nehis for Cuz and me.

Then turning her for home
He'd shout, Let the Speckled fly!
Sixty-one, two, three and Sixty-four.
That's all your miles per hours, boys,
She won't do any more.

He is pushing at the wheel.
We did not think he'd lie.
But now that I am a daddy,
I understand just why.

When you got a wife and children,
You can't leave it on the track.
You got to think about tomorrow.
You got to hold a little back.

And anyway, that truck did fly.
Daddy didn't tell a lie.
All that's in the eye you know.
The eye,
Of the beholder.

Chevy pickup truck for sale, Sampit, S.C

Bucksport Grocery with its many directives, near Bucksport, S.C.

FIRST

See! Out there
Where the last ever guano
Has been spread.
There. There. There it is!
The first infernal automobile
Comes rolling by the highway field.
The burble and clank,
The whiffling wail and rank smoke
Which comes from bore and stroke
Tossing in together. Tantalizing.
I mean we want to see it coming,
Be the first, embrace whatever new sharp end
They've whittled on the stick.
Still and all,
This was ease and abomination,
Backbone of our nation, churning by,
And yes, linked in tandem.
Dogs, boys, your great-grandfather, him
With derby hat cocked back.
On that day, they've seen the future.
Who knows if it works.

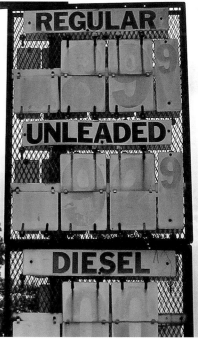

Service station memorabilia, Galivants Ferry, Nesmith, and Rhems, S.C

Beehives, spreading oak and Volkswagen stand in a field, Alvin, S.C.

LAST MAN STANDING

You'll need a car that's near all hood.
And make it black, black is good.
Yeah, a Hudson. That would do.
A '51 or '52.
Then park it under the big pecan.
That's the one. The front field.
Put my ashes in a tin.
Stick that behind the wheel.
Naugh. Roll down a window.
Let the chickens in.
No need to scrape. No need to bow,
Certainly no need to mourn
When the ghost of Annalee drives by,
She can blow the horn.

Junk yard sign near Felderville, S.C.

Paint fades on this Stars and Stripes sign, Dorchester, S.C.

This is the hymn of emptied lands
Sung as long-dead troops march by
Shoulder to shoulder they go.
There beneath gray skies where the pine woods sigh
This is the call of the chuck-will's-widow
Where the bays of the swamp spread wide
Over the slush of a vanished road
Where the ghosts of hard men stride.
from "The Blue and the Gray: A Song for Ted D."

Vine-covered silo stands in harvested soybean field, Holly Hill, S.C.

Flag-draped church window, Eutawville, S.C.

THE BLUE AND THE GRAY: A SONG FOR TED D.

The magazines speak of where we should go
And the billboards of roadside frills.
But nowhere is there mention of the hard men who were killed.
We won't hear of them from the speeding car
Nor feel an artillery's thunder.
And the soybean fields are no substitute
For battlefields surrendered.

Damn yellow flies and the creek did rise
and the rifle's fearsome crack
And there's a harsher note from the rough Sergeant's throat,
in those days of way, way back.
Bloody foot by foot, they moved that line,
till the line would move no longer
And those who led the charge lay down
when death proved out the stronger.

Gone are breastworks of rambling poles,
and forts of woods and thickets.
But there's a stretch by the Interstate they still call the "bloody picket"
(One famed for speeding tickets.)
No wild-eyed men with sabers to dodge.
No coffee ground from chicory.
We've seen the last of all that kind.
McDonald's has bested history.

This is the hymn of emptied lands
Sung as long-dead troops march by
Shoulder to shoulder they go.
There beneath gray skies where the pine woods sigh.
This is the call of the chuck-will's-widow
Where the bays of the swamp spread wide
Over the slush of a vanished road
Where the ghosts of hard men stride.

At the Feeder

Filling the bird feeder isn't the
Mightiest of human endeavors
But it is toward the top,
An offering to the sky gods,
A mild fever in the blood, a jealous nod.
Why were you and not me chosen
To rise and plummet,
To nudge the clouds and intercept the rain?

Audubon wrote his friend Bachman
Of the two white pelicans
He shot here on the south end of the bay.
They'd strayed far up the coast
And since the saying went
What's missed is mystery,
He shot them dead and said
Yes, two white pelicans.

Then Audubon's sons married
Bachman's daughters,
One of whom died and Audubon fell
To taking whiskey. He drank and drank
And did not paint and Bachman in despair
Shouted, Oh, you fool,
Had I the wings
How I would soar.

Dried Daisy

Dried daisy stuck between the pages,
Tannic scar of stem discarded,
Two clover blooms, pressed and faded,
Dent the paper. Someone once
Took pen in hand. Black ink now faint
Describes divisions, stamen, pistil.
But all I see is blooming ancients
Of a fallen grassy nation,
Wilted fragments of a field
Sunless, scentless, sealed in study,
They sing no more of May.

Oh, if I could catalogue her,
Count the ways, compare her to
A summer's day — she is more temperate.
Then apply to old Linnaeus.
Four limbs and flowering parts
That draw us in and stay between us.

Graveyard carving, St. Stephen, S.C.

The War

Silvered by a moonlight's touch;
Eyes of blue — pearls and frills.
A pleading of the waltz that thrills.
Doubt you some, know this much
A mix of wine and witchery
The blush of sweet sincerity
Says boys this brave can never die.

Men to the left, women right
Eyes of black — a throbbing reel.
Let parted lovers now unite.
Let bright hope rule the darkening sky.
Death, that master of disguise,
Says boys this brave can never die
While stars they sweep and wheel and fly.

Eyes rimmed with red — a dusty feign
On roads ablaze with summer heat,
Striking hoof and tightened rein,
A bugle call, a drum that beats.
A banner bold before them flies,
Tell we now that old, old lie?
Say boys this brave can never die?

Yes, you may claim its metaphor.
Shot through the heart,
They just lay down to rise once more.
At morning light shake off the grave
Go off again to whip Old Abe.
That's the South like it was before.
Alive with death and metaphor.

Happy St. Patrick's Day, Choppee, S.C.

SOMEWHERE OUT THERE
Somewhere out there waiting
Is a voice I haven't heard.
My aching heart's not broken,
Until she says those words.

Somewhere may be near here
Or somewhere off a ways
Across the road or outta state
Waits that heartbreak day.

Somewhere out there waiting
A face I'm going to see
My aching heart's not broken
Not like its going to be.

Somewhere may be near here,
Or off ten thousand miles.
Just now I might've seen her
She has a heartbreak smile.

Somewhere's right beside me.
Yes she's standing next to me.
A crime to be so happy.
This woman's all I need.

I won't be crossing lands
Or swimming foreign seas
She's moved in across the road
How easy this will be.

Somewhere out there waiting
Was that woman meant for me.
My aching heart won't break,
That's not how it's gonna be.

74

Highway 45 comes to an end and offers a magnificent view of this old house, Wells, S.C.

Doorway to Prince Frederick Parish Church, Georgetown, S.C

Shuttered window and faint drawing of woman, Strawberry Chapel, near Cordesville, S.C.

CHURCH RECORDS

After moving the church from Brown's Wolf Trap
To here on the King's Highway and before the war
That drove the King's men
From these shores,
That's when Widow Chicken
Had her bastard babies.
Some would say
No better than a whore,
Except all of them were Christened.
We have the records still.
Each year she came and made her mark.
I've touched the dust thick lines.

Thomas Lynch, among the great and few
Who signed for independence,
Signed his pew door too,
Then disappeared at sea
And left no Lynch behind.
Chickens though we had 'em.
Hardy Churchmen stock,
Each girl as pretty as her mama,
Each boy a credit to some papa.
Maybe one of these was Lynch's.
Little Thomas Chicken,
Conceived behind the church when
Spring did bring a quickening.
Yes, something there of Henry Fielding.
Fine lace cuffs and wench's yielding.
How sad for us who dream and wonder,
Not one hint in the priest's slim creeding.

Light and shadows, St. James, Santee Church, McClellanville, S.C.

Strawberry Chapel at Childsbury, near Cordesville, S.C.

Biggin Church gate, Moncks Corner, S.C.

I Had Expected

I had expected more of the afterlife,
A bright blue sky and a million zillion
white rocking chairs, all porch-bound
and in a line, creaking out in unison.
Maybe mountains in the distance.
Flat Rock, North Carolina
Scaled to heavenly proportions.
Of course, for the less deserving
There'd be that dark place, dark
As a midnight storm on a black sea,
Except when lightning forks
Prodded backsides
Making sinners shout and holler lies
And weep out fire from wicked eyes.
But no. On passing I have seen no such sights,
No endlessly rocking rocking chairs
Or fires in the black serving multitudes.
Might be so some other place,
But here, it's just us lively few.
We play a game of hide and seek
And maybe chase 'cause you can't say who
Is it and who isn't or exactly what's
Expected of the ones who win or lose.
Seems there is a garden,
Camellias with petals falling down,
down, and the scent of tea olive at
Twilight. The fireflies blink, and blink, and blink.
We whisper and we laugh
But in a disembodied way.
Some sing, some reach out, touch.
We're all together here,
Me, my sisters, and my cousins.
Seems we've had our supper
But bedtime never comes.

Passing

A storm's reluctant light,
The surf a demon's roar,
Two women dressed in blue
Standing on the shore.
One lights a cigarette,
Hands cupped as if in prayer,
The second tosses ashes
While wading to her knees.
Substance of the dead
On a now disrupted sea.
Oh, the vastness of her actions,
The smallness that we leave.

Requiem

Say no more of disbelief.
Lay still, lay still.
Don't make a fuss.
By God's hand you were made from dust
Or found by your mama 'neath a cabbage leaf.
Either way you've done enough
Lay still, lay still.
Don't make a fuss.

Tomb and church ruins, Sheldon, S.C.

Chapel's steeple, McClellanville, S.C.

Julie

Instead of sleep, the radio. It plays.
Last night there was a woman on
Who sees the guardian angels
Which keep each of us from harm.
When I sleep, I dream.
I run, kick, scream,
Knock pictures from the wall.
Where's mine?
Is she there through *all*
The night? Does she sleep
When I sleep and dream
Those same dreams, too?

When They

When they beat their breasts,
Angels rise into the air.
The motion of their arms
Brings the wings to bear.
Like the shaking of your head
Turns your lips into a smile.
And I'm certain of a laugh
For those hinge to each denial.

Thoughts on Autumn

My Celtic forefathers
Had a fondness for
Blue body paint and mistletoe
And murder for no reason,
Drank to stupefaction and
Worshipped God knows what
Incarnations of the Devil.
We might think we live in scary times,
Read the headlines,
Imagine everyday is Halloween.
Still and all, things could be worse
You know it's true,
For in the course of what is mystery
What is likely will be.
So, here's my plan:
"The Grand Plan."
Rake the lawn,
Burn the leaves,
Stare into the demon trees
And hold my breath 'til Sunday.

Behind the House

I don't care.
Maybe E does equal
MC square.
Fine for the earth
To go 'round the sun
And all life here
To be the grand sum
Of heated pond scum.
Can't help myself.
I'm still searching for that
Middle ground,
Some magic spot
Out past the pond
But in line with
Lee's deer stand.
Yes. To the sweet
Gum tree. At least that far.
You see, I need the land
To swell beneath my feet,
To bulge pear shaped,
To raise me on my way,
And when I look straight up,
Light comes sprinkling
From the backyard stars.

Oak

That's the Cornwallis oak,
There, leading to the cemetery.
Ten feet across with drooping limbs.
Dates back to a time when
We weren't free,
Back to when
Generals stood under trees
And ordered men to fight
For God, King, Country, what was right,
To leave Piccadilly
And go be buried
In unmarked graves
Beyond the cemetery,
Bayoneted,
Picnicked on,
And forgotten.

Methodist church, Lone Star, S.C.

Prince Frederick Parish Church, Georgetown, S.C.

Ruins of Old Sheldon Church, Sheldon, S.C.

Statue at St. Matthews Lutheran Church, Creston, S.C.

AT THE BAPTISM

Reverend Prentiss, the palmist,
He baptized our Sara.
He was an educated man, some said wise.
After the service he held her a second time. Here, he said,
This line is for a long life. As the palm was tiny,
We must see it in proportion to the whole. And
Here, she will marry a good man.
See, three children. Count them. One, two, three.
She is very happy. And this...I cannot say what
That might bring. Nor should we ask all of the stars.
And strangely, she did have the three,
And then the fourth and was happier than ever.

Target United Methodist Church and graveyard, Holly Hill, S.C.

St. Stephen's Parish Church, St. Stephen, S.C.

Marble columns in Hopewell Presbyterian Church graveyard, near Claussen, S.C.

A Musical Brocade

When man first came to church did he
Stride, bow, shuffle, kneel, cough and pray?
And did he sing no semblance of a tune
When in the hymnal he could find
That thin line of musical brocade
And make some sense of what the organ played?
Did he hum low for the rest?
Did his wife think that song of his a test
Of testament and all the rest.
And love him all the same?
If so:
As she was the second being to attend
Let her be forgiven elbows to his side
And all other efforts to condemn
Those joyous outpouring and solemn
Chants in which God took such pride.

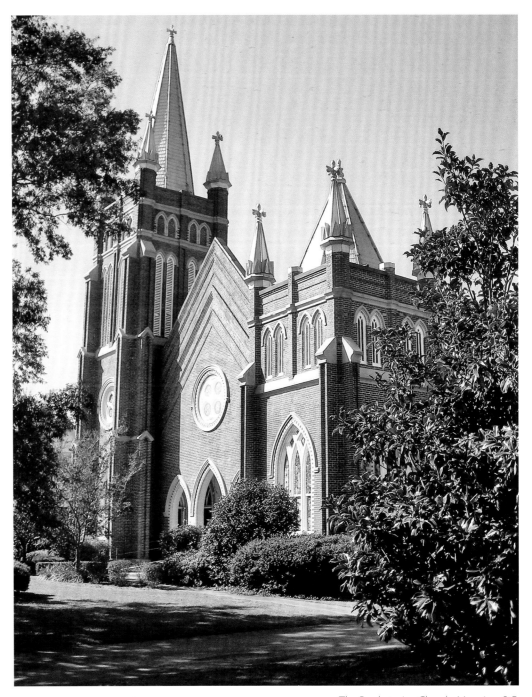

The Presbyterian Church, Manning, S.C.

87

I DREAM OF YOU

In dreams of sleep, I dream of you
How deep is love, how deep, deep, deep.
But was that love or something else?
Gotta find out for myself.

Dreamed I called you yesterday.
To say "hello" before you go.
And by the time you answered me,
We said goodbye once more.

Dreamed you called me yesterday.
You said hello that same old way
But by the time I answered you
That yes had gone away.

I sleep to dream
I dream of you
I need a book
To say this means
And draw out
Complicated schemes
Do's and don't's
Fronts and backs
The girl said this
the boy said that.
A masterpiece to explain
Complaining
You're not here.

I met you at I can't say where.
By yourself. You'd just got there.
In dreams I see you everywhere.
I know just why that is.

You rinsed both cups out in your sink.
You turned the mattress over.
Seemed the start of something big
Something to get over.

I sleep to dream
I dream of you
I need a book
To say this means
And draw out
Complicated schemes
Do's and don't's
Fronts and backs
The girl said this
The boy said that.
A masterpiece to explain
Complaining
You're not here.

I can't take this booth no more.
Take me onto the dance floor.
A corner where the light's not bright.
I want to dance tonight.

Spend your quarter and play our song.
The one I'm planning in my head
The one that takes my breath away
And fills the ice trays up.

I sleep to dream
I dream of you
I need a book
To say this means
And draw out
Complicated schemes
Do's and don't's
Fronts and backs
The girl said this
The boy said that.
A masterpiece to explain
Complaining
You're not here.

In dreams of sleep, I dream of you
How deep is love, how deep, deep, deep.
But was that love or something else?
Gotta find out for myself.

Ocean Bay swamp lilies, Halfway Creek, S.C.

Shrimp boat high and dry, Awendaw, S.C.

STORM

A racquet. I took that
And hugged the tree.
My right hand
Held the grip,
Strings the left.
Sis, I said, Sis,
Hold on to me.
Hold tight.
She did. She held me
Fierce and tight and
As the water rose
We rose
And as the water fell
We fell.
My arms were
Bloody raw,
And where the racquet rode,
The bark was gone.

Fish market door with swordfish, Conway, S.C.

Signs along roadside advertise fish bait and produce, Conway, S.C.

MAN IS

Man is the naming animal,
Endowed by God for the purpose
And of late amiss.
Let's crank time back to Genesis.
Let dire wolves again be dire
And cats have saber teeth.
In days of yore we understood the power
Of names. The wooly mammoth
Was both wooly and mammoth.
Go back, go back, go back
Until bandicoots are again
Pig-footed.
And naming man is just a thing,
Poor, forked, predatory,
But God-driven and possessed by poetry.

Taxidermist and storekeeper Dan Daniels behind the counter of his unusual bait and tackle shop, Low Falls Landing, S.C.

Stuffed bear greets visitors, Low Falls Landing, S.C.

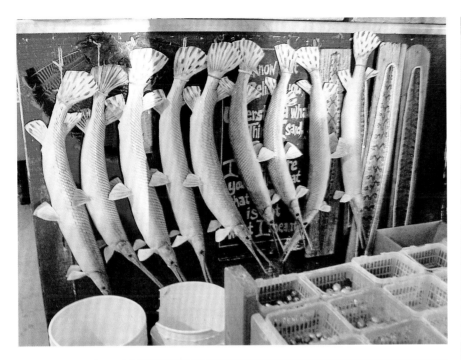

Interior of Mr. Daniels' shop, Low Falls Landing, S.C.

Corbett Smith displays his new treasure, a gator's head, McClellanville, S.C.

HIM: OLD SONG

I sing the body electric.
That's an old, old song.
Something the Captain shouted
When something small went wrong.
He was a gunner and a fisherman
And ran a boat, as well.
All across this village
He cast a marveling spell.
Just to be beside him,
That was all it took.
Enough to smell tobacco
And watch him bait a hook.
Father of my mother,
He stays a part of me.
One step in a procession,
Towards eternity.

HER: OLD SONG

I sing the body electric.
That's an old, old song.
Something the Captain whispered
When grandmamma was along.
She was a lover. She was a mother
And kept a shop, as well.
All across this village
She cast a marveling spell.
Just to be beside her,
That was all it took.
Enough to smell her powder
And watch her crochet hook.
Mother of my mother,
She stays a part of me.
One step in a procession,
Towards eternity.

TIMMY'S WALKER
Crossed one county line
And headed for more
Lord, dog, what I get you for.
Just bury me on the rice field stand
Put the Browning Silver in my hand
Then let him out and shout
Run, Bob, run.
Yep. I've seen the sun
Set on my last loose Walker hound.
But I'll listen up in Heaven,
'Cause I do love the sound.

Clubhouse, Chicken Creek Gun Club, Honey Hill, S.C.

Skulls and skeletons create an eerie entrance to this country property, Elloree, S.C.

SALVATION

Now Mama, now Mama
Tell me what is real.
I see buildings crumbling
And What should I feel?
Jesus in the tomb.
Mary Magdalene
On the way.
Lord sent down an angel
To roll that stone away.
Roll that stone away, Lord,
Roll that stone away.

From high and low finance,
Proud heart, rebellious brow
Deaf ears and souls uncaring,
Lord, we seek protection now.
Yes, People, dear people,
Let's fold our hands and pray
That sweet Mary comes searching
And That stone gets rolled away.

Now Papa, now Papa,
Can all this be true
I see children starving
Cause trucks can't get through.
Jesus in the tomb.
Mary Magdalene
On the way.

Lord sent down an angel
To roll that stone away.
Roll that stone away, Lord,
Roll that stone away.

Earth that boils with anger
A sea that's dark with wrath
The nations of those others
They keep standing in our path.
Before we loose legions
Before we pull the blade.
Let's fold our hands and pray
That that dark and mighty stone
It gets rolled far, far away.

Now Mama, now Mama
Tell me what is real.
I see buildings crumbling
And What should I feel?
Jesus in the tomb.
Mary Magdalene
On the way.
Lord sent down an angel
To roll that stone away.
Roll that stone away, Lord,
Roll that stone away.

Revival tent, Jamestown, S.C.

Collapsing farmhouse, Martin Corner, S.C.

Barn at edge of pine woods, Georgetown, S.C.

Sans Paint

A house that goes unpainted
For a man that doesn't care.
It's well beyond the roadside
A place to step with care.
Got the mattress in the kitchen,
The porch is pulled away,
The roof is losing shingles,
The windows dirty gray.
He's lost the will to paint that house
And the need to love her too,
But she's coming by tomorrow
And she claims she'll pull them through.

Lost fields that go unplowed
By a man that doesn't care.
Twenty acres gone to pines
Remainder close to bare.
The tractor needs both tire and rim.
The harrows been laid to rest.
But she's got her hand in his.
And she is saying:
Listen. Listen. God knows best.
Now he's got his arms around her.
And he is smiling through his tears.
Love can't paint a house,
But it will bind our deepest fears.

Log barn at former pig farm, St. Stephen, S.C.

Tobacco barn with classic sloping roof design, near Mullins, S.C.

Graceful roof line of barn, Wells, S.C.

WIDOW WOMAN, WILL YOU MARRY ME?

Seven years, at last you're free.
Widow woman will you marry me?
It's not his tractor, it's not his plow.
I loved you then and I love you now.
It's not his tools, it's not his boat.
They declared him dead, that's all she wrote.
It's you I love and it's you I need.
He was a trifling bastard and now you're freed.

(Chorus)
If hell was close as Texas,
He'd have found his way back home.
That's why I'm certain, certain, certain,
That he's gone, gone, gone.
Seven years. At last you're free.
Widow woman,
Will you marry me?

103

Heavenly fuel, Bloomingvale, S.C.

LINES FOR ALICE

The dead are always with us
For they live in every smile.
They put the salt in tear drops
And arms 'round every child.
They're grateful for the privilege
And give credence to our trust
That love extends beyond the bounds
Of what we think is us.

Rusty water pump in field, Nesmith, S.C.

Cotton basket adorns wall, Lane, S.C.

Country store at end of dirt road near the railroad crossing, Foreston, S.C.

Storms have blown away most of the tin to reveal an older shingle roof below, Johnsonville, S.C.

SWEET NEGLECT

Bathrobe loose, hair still free,
Sweet neglect, she's what she'll be.
House-bound lover, farm run down.
No planting now, just fallow ground.

I am two fools, I guess you know
For loving you and saying so.
She gave a look, washed her face,
Then tidied up around the place.

Again his eyes caressing go
Before, behind, above, below.
Here she is, his new found land.
It's chore enough for any man.

She says they'll see what they will see.
Again there's talk of that old movie.
Breathless where the French gets spoken
And the hero's heart gets broken.

The guy in that, he steals a car.
Girl turns him in, he don't get far.
Did she love him? Who can say?
Fools don't come 'round every day.

Foreign films put all in doubt.
No tomatoes to set out.
Lord, sell this farm, the planet's spent.
Like the French, just pay some rent.

Doorway looking out on a crop of corn, near Kingstree, S.C.

Wagon wheel in need of repair, Mullins, S.C.

THE LONESOME COWBOY

As a child
I had my heart set on
Cowboying,
Lonesome cowboying,
To be exact.
Me on my palomino
Me, just so, with hat pulled down hard,
And held in place with a narrow strip of blanket.
Yeah, I'd ride the fence. Hunched low, I'd go.
I'd patch the wire, keep the posts upright,
And sleep out in the snow
On those nights, when lost and wandering, the blinding blizzard
Kept me from the line shack that was my lonesome home.
Lofty ambitions for a young soul.
Who's never even touched a horse
Or seen a flake of snow.
Knowing what I know now,
I mean having seen cows standing off in fields,
Seen them from behind the safety of a windshield,
Or trimmed and grilled and set down before me on a plate
And having often enough stood alone in the house
Wondering where you are,
I realize lonesome cowboying
Was a poor first choice
And I'm toying with the notion
Of a kiss.

Skinny nag, Jamestown, S.C.

Darkness over silos and train cars, Vance, S.C.

Dairy cows and silver silos, Providence, S.C.

Tiny peach stand, Rome, S.C.

Barn full of baskets, near Wells, S.C.

GOBLIN STAND

Was Halloween of fifty four,
Sixty years plus some more
Liz and Laura took their drive
In Daddy's plush sedan —
That Blue Buick with a chrome band
Anyway, they pass a stand.
Fresh produce here. Gourds on high.
Honest weights. Square dealings.

Our Laura spun the wheel around,
She'd heard the goblin's cry:
Come buy. Come buy our orchard fruits,
Come buy. Come buy. Come buy:
Apples, pecans, watermelons,
Firm and downy peaches,
Peanuts parched, peanuts boiled,
All grown in Southern soil

Turnips and cabbage, Pee Dee region, S.C.

Pumpkins, limas, honeydew,
Potatoes, collards too.
Figs to fill your longing mouth.
Square. Honest. Don't you doubt,
Sweet to tongue and sweet to eye
Come buy. Come buy. Come buy.
Don't look. Don't look, Lizzie cried,
And turns her head away.

We must not look at goblin men
We must not buy their fruits
Who know upon what soil they fed
Their hungry thirsty roots?
Again she cried, Don't look! Don't look!
Then Laura she forsook.
 A dimpled finger in each ear,
 She shut her eyes and ran.

She left sedan and sister there.
Laura chose to linger.
And wondered at each farmstand man.
Three came with tails of fur,
One had the odd face of a bat,
One had the look of lover.
Laura stretched her neck far out,
A gentle floating swan,

Cigar Man, Santee Circle, S.C.

A stainless vessel at the launch
When last restraint is gone.
The goblin men gave their shrill cry,
Come buy, come buy, come buy.
On all sides they stood stock still.
Leering at each other,
Brother, Brother with sly brother.
One set his basket down.

He then began to weave a crown
Of leaves and vines around.
Come buy, come buy was still their cry.
Our Laura pleaded thus.
I have no dollars in my purse,
I have no silver either,
You have gold curls upon your head,
They answered all together.

She clips a precious lock for them.
Then ate their fruit of care.
She never tasted such before.
She ate and ate the more
Of love that unknown orchards bore.
Ate until her stomach pained.
Then flung the emptied rinds away.
Yet kept one bitter pit.

You see, it was her heart she held.
Shrunk and turned to stone.
For goblins are just what they seem.
The same is true of men.

Mask on a porch, Cordesville, S.C.

Nevermore: the Song

Said the Raven on the bookcase,
To the poet in despair,
I came by much earlier
But I thought you'd gone somewhere.
I thought you'd gone to meet her,
Thought you'd drifted off in time,
You were thinking on her beauty
And went searching for a rhyme.
I guess I was napping
I told him in reply.
I didn't hear you tapping,
But that was just a lie.
Truth is:
I've had my fill of demons
And of situations fey.
I'm going to see a man
About a dog. Hey! Listen.
A pup's going to cure me.
I know I'm going to mend.
Goodbye to you, Raven
I'll be talking to a friend.

Seagulls hate me, McClellanville, S.C.

The Poet

It's just ten cents, the poet's dime
Same as yours. See, same as mine.
Pains forgotten. Pains subdued.
I drag them up to be renewed.
Joys forgotten, those, too.
And Joys subdued.
I pull them out to be reviewed.
That same old dime I spend again
And when you think it's gone, is when
I take it out to spend again.

Welcome sign, Russellville, S.C.

MAN-EATING MEETING

A question that's come through the ages
One certain to draw remarks:
When a man-eating woman
Meets a man-eating shark,
Is it love at first sight,
Or love at first bite,
Or something that's done in the dark?

I can readily cite you an instance
A sexy young lady but mean
neither tender nor sweet
a breaker of hearts,
Fell in the bar with a scream.

She struggled and flounced on the dance
floor,
And signaled in vain to the bar,
And she'd surely been raved
if she hadn't been saved
By a chivalrous man-eating shark.

He bowed in a manner most polished
Soothing her impulses wild.
Then he offered his fin
She took fin and him
While speaking, he gave a broad smile

The most chivalrous fish of the ocean
To ladies forebearing and mild,
Though the record be dark,
We man-eating sharks,
Will eat neither woman nor child.

Of course, the patrons all cheered
And drinks were raised in salute.
So don't be frightened, he said.
Plus, I've recently fed.
She said, What a beautiful suit.

When a man-eating woman
Meets a man-eating shark,
Is it love at first sight,
Or love at first bite?
Or something that's done in the dark?

I wish I had you an answer
I wish it was "yes" or "no."
But they left the bar
I think they went far.
As a couple they seemed content.
Life is a place of mysteries
And half of it's spent in the dark.

Store front window advertises musical entertainment, Elloree, S.C.

Effie Road, Shulerville, S.C.

ODDS AND ENDS
Add 'em up
Odds and ends
Equating to oblivion.
Oceans rise,
Planets spin
Light goes straight
Then it bends.

Christ, the Master,
Hear this prayer.
Make our lives
A world contained
By Vital Love
And Care.

Paradise
Lost again
Jesus merely history.
Gone is all
The splendor.
Gone from us
Sweet mystery.

Christ, the Master,
Hear this prayer.
Make our day
A world sustained
By Vital Love
And Care.

What's bright
An' beautiful
What's dark and awkward too
Dappled white
Pit of night
We fashion
What is true.

Christ, the Master,
Hear this prayer.
Make each hour
A world contained
By Vital Love
And Care.

Hell we make
From heaven
But just the odds and ends
Love does rise
Doubts descend
We understand
What's gained.

Christ, the Master,
Hear this prayer.
Make each breath
A world contained
By Vital Love
And Care.

120

Juke joint down dirt road, Greeleyville, S.C.

Unfinished renovations on a grand old house, Greeleyville, S.C.

For Kathy L.

The flag has been folded
There's still time to cry.
When the coffin was lowered
I heard her whisper goodbye.
Now, with Tennyson we've crossed the bar.
Ten years. Less or maybe more.
I guess we'll find out just how far
It is our pilot/maker waits.
With that house of many mansions,
In that Love of grand dimensions.
For now she'll be my angel
And I'll go and find some lunch.

State tree adorns wrought iron gate, St. Matthews, S.C.

CADILLAC MAN
Bible rich
Meets Bible poor
The Cadillac man
At our front door.
Where's your mama?
Is she out back?
Ohio.
I think it was Ohio.
Or some other place far off
Where only God can find her
And His Love don't have a cost.

Faded paint offers an oval image where a mirror once hung, Millwood Community, S.C.

Pears are plentiful in this lady's yard, Greeleyville, S.C.

Victorian house with double porches, Holly Hill, S.C.

A LITTLE BIT OF DONNE
Of many spheres one heaven's made
One robin brings the spring
For all's in one and one's in all
God's love equates all things

Christmas balls hang from cedar limbs, McClellanville, S.C.

School desk at Home Charity Lodge, Cross, S.C.

LUNCH AT T. W. GRAHAM'S WITH SAM AND ANNE KNIGHT AND OH, YEAH, BUD WAS THERE

First you love and then you lose.
You heard it here, read it there.
Some such wisdom's everywhere.
But each child born starts out new.
Chalks their slate just like you.
Two and two it's four again.
They learn their sixes and their tens.
They multiply, subtract, descend
Into a world where mad men
Make the rules then break them.

First she loves him, then she won't.
Their touches burn, then they don't.
Then he loves her, now he won't.
Do not shed but one more tear
And let that be the last one.
All races run, victories sung,
Our bodies to the dust declare
Fleshy lessons learned up here.
Gather rosebuds while you may,
Clip coupons, save away.

Don't go now expecting more
Heaven's door sprung from hinges
Cherubims to clap rhythms.
Oil they drill beneath our feet
Bombs are busting overhead
They made land and sea a sieve.
The sky a dismal place of dread.
War and wealth should halt in place
So those on earth may humbly
Bow and pray, beg for grace.

First you love and then you lose.
You heard it here, read it there.
Some such wisdom's everywhere.
Six o'clock the news comes on.
There's so much beauty to erase.
Dogs in mangers, dervish whirls,
And deadly stuff to store some place.
I'll ink it down on narrow scroll
There's nothing helps but love,
That and growing old.

Former schoolhouse and church building being restored, Cherry Hill, S. C.

Rehoboth Methodist Church, Macbeth, S.C.

WITH GOD

His the grace of summer day.
Ours the bee
And ours the bonnet.
Ours the ever arching
Need.
His the rainbow set upon it.
Ours the shout.
His the sun.
Fifty-fifty. Not exactly.
Ninety-nine and ours the one.

Wrought iron encloses family plot at St. Matthew's Lutheran Church graveyard, Creston, S.C.

Old Bethel A.M.E. Church, McClellanville, S.C.

Alice, a fence go up.
All around a fence go up.
I don't feel that pain no more.
That white nurse, that little one,
She whisper, Margarite, what happen here?
I say, you know God?
She say, yeah, I know God.
I say, God happen here.
Now I home. God come at night. He say,
Margarite, what you worry for, Margarite?
Alice, God got a deep, deep voice.
I not afraid anymore. I going to Heaven.
from "Margarite"

Wind lifts roof tin at Taveau Church, Cordesville, S.C.

Abandoned church, Halfway Creek, S.C.

GOD'S LOVE

God's Love is wider than the sky
For put them side by side,
The one the other will include
With ease and us beside.
(Chorus)

Sing praise to God who holds us
God of all creation.
God of power and God of Love.
God of our Salvation.

God's Love is deeper than the sea
For hold them, blue to blue,
The one the other will absorb,
And drain the rivers too.
(Chorus)

God's Love is brighter than the sun.
For place them end to end,
And the sun will cast a shadow
As we the sun commend.
(Chorus)

God's Love is gentler than the dew
For lay them on a bloom.
The one the other will console
As sorrows are assumed.
(Chorus)

God's Love is longer than our reach.
For stretch them out apart
The one the other will enclose
And still embrace our heart.
(Chorus)

Old Eccles Church and cross, near Huger, S.C.

135

Small praise house, McClellanville, S.C.

GARDEN

Imagine that, we men alone.
God of love with blessed might,
What is tempered holds the light.
Spit there where the flame is hottest.
Bend, stamp, fold and spindle
Precious flesh by sin unknown.
From Adam's side, knead and kindle
Walking, talking honeycombs.
Imagine that, we men alone.
Old Rock and Roll's sweet miracle,
Your blush, your breath, which God enjoins.

Statue of Mary, near Ridgeland, S.C.

Outhouse at Indian Fields, St. George, S.C.

HYMN VERSE
From our wants be unfettered.
God is big and more's the better
When you touch on love.

For all the rest, we need much less.
They coax and sing, these plastic things
Go and live without them.

Perish every fond ambition
See how rich is your condition.
God in Heaven can't be owned.

Indian Fields Methodist Campground, St. George, S.C.

Old Bethel's steeple, McClellanville, S.C.

MAGARITE

Margarite is in our house,
She who with Southern darkie wiles,
Coaxed me into helping her
Make Mama's beds, cook and clean,
and love her with my otherwise
Indulged white heart.
And what was house work, anyway.
She'd raise that quick brown hand,
Snap finger to thumb,
And make her popping sound.
Ain't nothing to 'em.
Not the way I do 'em.
Oh, blessed angels in Heaven above.

Hush. Hush. Iron in hand,
Margarite demands
Quiet For her soaps, her stories,
Those outlandish contraptions of
Afternoon TV which pale so in comparison
To what she would live as wife, mother,
Sister, sighing, laughing confronter.
Hush, Alice, Hush.
Those programs
No match even for my own endurings.
Not close.

At us both, child and maid, here comes life.
That shuffle on the back porch, a whoop,
It crowds against the screen door.
Wet from falling in the creek,
Snot nosed, hungry, and all unscripted.
Margarite at 53,
Me at 46.
Alice, I got cancer. You think I goin die?
No! I say No!
And all at once there're breasts removed.
I so scarred. That one in the other bed
She die. Early they come and take her out.
Zip her in the bag real quiet.
I hear that sound
And I so scarred.
Alice, them white doctor and nurse,
They gather round my bed.
They say Mrs. Gaethers this
and Mrs. Gaethers that.
Alice, my mind tell me, Margarite,
They talking 'bout putting them back on.

I tell 'em,
I had them thing a long time.
I have shown 'em off
But I don't need that, not no more.
And she is laughing. Laughing.
Then I see her in her car.
These grans, I taking them to Walmart.
Oh, Alice, my head bald as a baby's behind
For me there's just time to give a kiss
And see one rag tied around her head
Two more tucked into her bra.

And now, again comes the pain
They got a long needle
That go down in my lung.
I ain't never feel such. Never, ever.
Alice, I start saying the 23rd Psalm.
The Lord my Shepherd, I shall not want!
I see tears come rolling down her cheeks.
Alice, a fence go up.
All around a fence go up.
I don't feel that pain no more.
That white nurse, that little one,
She whisper, Margarite, what happen here?
I say, you know God?
She say, yeah, I know God.
I say, God happen here.
Now I home. God come at night. He say,
Margarite, what you worry for, Margarite?
Alice, God got a deep, deep voice.
I not afraid anymore. I going to Heaven.

I tell them young girl in the Church
They tease me,
Say, Margarite, how you know?
I say, I going. And I going into heaven,
Laughing and singing, too.

Her son Dennis standing close.
Her daughter's there. Linda.
An army nurse who's served in places far away.
So precious to Margarite, as are they all.
I sat on the bed and whispered,
Margarite.
Who you? She wonders. I don't know you.
I took her face in my hands.
Well, I know you!
Oh, Alice, Alice.

4 a.m. the phone.
Margarite has passed.
Linda asks,
Do I want to see the body?
With first light breaking,
They come in groups of two and three,
Beneath the limbs of oaks,
Neighbors, family, friends
Walk toward her house.
Voices murmur, footsteps on the road,
Inside a quiet vigil kept.
Linda steps with such grace
Through the bedroom door,
Invites me back to sit with her,
To sit with Dennis
On bed edge. The bed shared

With Margarite one last time.
We talk. How strange. We talk.
And Margarite is so beautiful,
All pain wiped away.
Her face smooth.
Her body slender young.
She looks sixteen, again.
Coming through our door
Each morning, Sixteen
And come to clean
And teach me
How to be a human being.
Goodbye to them.

I went out to the car.
Sat with fingers gripping at the wheel
And wondered what God had in mind
To take our Margarite this way.
Tears delayed. We weep for selves
As well as others. Weep when
All that story of our lives
Contrives to break into that fragile
Shell we call ourselves.
Alice. Alice.
Listen. Alice.
Margarite? She's in the car.
Alice.
Margarite? You're here.
Alice, all that I went through,
Ain't nothing to em
Went just like that. Alice. Just like that.
She made that popping sound.

Brown Angel's thumb to finger snaps.
Went just like that Alice. Just like that.
Oh, Margarite. I'm so glad it did.
Alice, God got a deep, deep, voice.
He say, Margarite, you here.
Alice, I am.

Magnolia blossom, Cope, S.C.

Drugstore sign, Marion, S.C.

Block glass window, Mayesville, S.C.

MAIN STREET

When they cut the bypass
They found the bones
Of little whales.
To build the Walmart
They paved my PaPa's place.
Plus I was born on Main Street.
I was baptized on Main Street.
I started school on Main Street.
I graduated on Main Street.
My mama and daddy are buried
In the graveyard there
On the end of Main Street.
So you ask:
What happened to Main Street?
That's a long story.

Hall's Dime Store Building, Elloree, S.C.

Town clock on Main Street, Elloree, S.C.

TOMORROW:
FOR ELIZABETH, HARV, AND JIMMY
They went so quickly
Those whose presence
Was a happy given.
For such vain presumptions
Be we now forgiven.

Let each remaining day
Be open to the claims
Of light triumphant
And recognize the shame
Of succoring delay.

THE HOLY CITY: FOR BEN, JIM AND DANNY
Who can say?
Not every church has a steeple
We could kneel
On Main Street. Let some pass
To the left
And some the right, casting as
They go looks of concern,
Amusement, annoyance,
Shout out our prayers
Or whisper what's required.
Who can say?
Not every Bible is a book.

Our souls roll off,
A river dark and flowing,
On the banks are roses, wild and pink and tumbling.
Then we breach a city street, truck besotted, rumbling.
Who's to know the half of it,
When grace is so obliging?

Decorated doorway, Kingstree, S.C.

Store windows, Holly Hill, S.C.

COUNTRY MATTERS

Ophelia don't go in there.
Hamlet's in a mood.
His daddy has been murdered
And you won't be getting wooed.
Listen, listen, Baby,
'Cause you can hear it all.
The Prince is laughing, laughing
In the room just down the hall.

You're honest and you're fair.
Be all his sins uncovered.
He claims God gave you one face
And you must paint another.
Listen, listen Baby,
'Cause you can hear it all.
He speaks of country matters
In that room just down the hall.

Don't lie with him tonight.
Don't lie with him tomorrow.
Listen to your daddy.
Do not lend and do not borrow.
Ophelia, save yourself for someone else.
Don't tickle the bee. Don't taste the honey
He loves you, he loves you not.
Keep it on the side that's sunny.

Keep on the sunny side.
Keep on the sunny side.
Keep on the sunny side of life.
It will help you every day.
It will brighten all your way.
If you keep on the sunny side of life.

Bullet holes dot store window, St. Stephen, S.C.

Remaining buildings of business district, Lone Star, S.C.

Lone Star

Will wonders never cease?
Driving up to what was Lone Star
Through the windshield I think I saw more
Grand strangeness than Hubble ever
Dreamed of with his tiny galaxies locked in tiny reels.
And in watching me pass through
Weren't you treated to the same?
Sin, cotton gins, and barbeque,
Love, marriage, children and even hate,
The grand debates of who did what to whom
And why God put us here
Then stuck heaven, hell and Georgia
Further down the line.
Are we the hope of destinations?
Part and parcel of Lone Star's imagination?
They say life is just a passage.
They say it was the train's
Single headlamp coming on the track,
A brief white light distant as a lone star, then
Growing, growing, growing bright
Pushing at the edge of a station master's night.
Four buildings, emptied of all purpose, still lit,
Still shaken by the roaring trains, still named
For distant, rushing light.

Store with overhanging roof, Lone Star, S.C.

Road to Davis Stores, Centenary, S.C.

WALKING THE DOG AND OTHER TRICKS

I took the dog and went
Into that world where life unfurls.
That place spent on dead ends
And common loss.
A hundred years and who will know
What mystery here curled
Among the bristling vines
Behind that lot.
She ran on knots.
Mister Skipper's Stanley.
No oil. Pine knots.
With steam up he drove her
Fast and free until dysentery
Broke man from machine.
The automobile,
Enshrouded in God's green
Gloom, was lost from view.
There is Mister Skipper's steamer.
There. Those who knew would say.
That heap of vines. She ran on knots
Of pine. Ran fine, they'd say. Until
At last (and long years passed)
The vines were clipped away.
No steamer. Not one bolt nor hint of ash.
And so it is with what came to pass.
There dog. There's your lesson.
Tomorrow: Time and what it's spent on.

Shadows on a small store and gas station, Jamestown, S.C.

Only vacant buildings remain, Mayesville, S.C.

No more seeds, Kingstree, S.C.

153

One of two vaults . . . all that's left of Alterman's Timber Mill building, Alcolu, S.C.

ALCOLU

He leaned against the deep worn counter, nursed his beer,
Said: You know the past is another land.
It's true. I've traveled there.
Ten miles from here, just down that way
Yes, Old State Road off 521, you'll come to Alcolu.
Place is like that poem they made us learn
Two giant stone feet and nothing else but sand.
See, a company town, that's Alcolu
Logging trains snaking through the woods,
Crossing swamps, rivers. Narrow tracks
Laid down all 'round and ending at the mill there,
Which some say was the second biggest anywhere.
You look on that and marvel
'Cept what's to see in Alcolu?
One long clapboard empty store
Where a man and his wife, too, once went to spend
The company chit, the babbit, it was called,
On food and clothing, and what you want, including one flight up,
A giant room to watch the movies in--
Him and her to sit and stare at something bright made of dreams.
There's that place and down the way the two strong vaults,
Like crypts those are. Mausoleums. And naked.
No building near. Just vaults and each taller than the tallest man.
Bold as business. Bare brick, iron doors with locks by Mosler Safe.
They'll open. Go and see. Pull hard and they'll swing free.
Shelf, on shelf, on shelf, it's true,
The company books, thick in dust, thick in mold, all enrolled,
Every inked-in entry's there, notes in passing, everlasting
Evidence of every single man and tree
That ever grew around Alcolu.

Alterman's Mill Store building with empty theater upstairs, Alcolu, S.C.

Shop sign and variety of machines, Awendaw, Shirley, and Andrews, S.C.

Perforated metal seat, Tibwin, S.C.

Pecan tree, McClellanville, S.C.

THE SINGER'S SONG

I've come into my own again,
Fed, forgiven and known again,
Claimed by bone, cheered by flesh.
Mama, your girl is home again.

No. Don't start. 'Cause my music mine.
I'm going leave this farm again.
No. Don't worry, I'll take some time.
But I am leaving this farm again.

Papa advises care,
Brother whispers prison,
And all I do is swear
When Mama Catechisms.

Fine welcome for the prodigal,
No damn rest for the weary gal.
It seems my mates are best for me,
Go back to the band unblessed?

Oh, if home was what it seemed
And not the home of dreams
But a place of boards and paint,
I'd leave right now,
But I know, Sweet Lord, it ain't.

They say I've gone and sold
A gift God only lent.
And talk of money spent
And talk of the pace I went.

Oh, Lord. Liquor and drugs.
Please no. Let's not go there.
I learned those lessons
And with lessons to spare.

Oh, if home was what it seemed
And not the home of dreams,
But a place of boards and paint.
I'd leave right now,
But I know, Sweet Lord, it ain't.
But I know, Sweet Lord, it ain't.
But I know, Sweet Lord, it ain't.

No, I won't be marrying.
At least not any time soon.
No grandbabies coming,
At least not any time soon.

Now thank you for the bed,
Now thanks for the meals.
Six pounds I've gained.
Can't tell you how it feels.

And I go as a Wiser Girl.
Not so easy to rob again
Or so ready to sob again
On any old neck that is there.

I'm off, Papa. Good-bye to you!
God bless, Mama I'll write to you!
Looks like I'm leaving home again.
Good Brother. Here's a song for you.

Oh, if home was what it seemed
And not the home of dreams,
But a place of boards and paint,
How quick I'd have left,
But you know, Sweet Bro, it ain't.

Cabin doorway, Cubbege Hill, S.C.

Hell Hole: the Symphony

At Halfway Creek you
Stopped to water horses
And checked the pistol flints,
'Cause this was Hell Hole,
A grand swampland,
Pocked with broad brambly circles
And darkly occupied.
Close by was Ahmen Crossing,
A quick sand bed now graded over
And changed to Farewell Corner.
They say beneath those oaks
General Francis Marion dismissed his troops
There being no Redcoats
Left to shoot.
Him, a small, hard man, swarthy complexed,
Wearing a blood-crusted
Dark green coat
And Prussian helmet with saber dent.
Not one to stand on
Formalities...
But the spot he said goodbye at
Was platted Farewell Creek
By Mr. Clement
Forty years before that war to
Make us free. Then
Starting in 1930, Us,
That same Government
Bought up most of Hell Hole.
My land and your land.
Grooming, blooming,
Some hiking and biking.
In Francis Marion *National* Forest.
Still, Tiger Swamp has panthers—

Maybe one or two.
True, the wolves that kept Mr. Clement
Treed for an entire night
Were eaten soon after by bears
And alligators.
Did you know
Hell Hole rattlesnakes can be
Mistaken for fallen logs?
Water moccasins fight razor-tusked hogs
And as for human kind:
When a slave had had enough,
Slipped his chains
And walked back to Africa,
This is where he went.
In there with them, and afterward,
Was every white felonious horse thief
Who wasn't caught and hanged.
Razorville to Scuffletown,
Entrepreneurs boiled out turpentine
And grew rice and chopped the forest down,
But no doubt about it, making
Corn liquor is what they did best.
At Sugar Swamp and Still Landing
Mason jars of it
Stacked up to the stars.
If ever there was a free country,
I mean one steeped in anarchy,
It'd be here.
I'll just say it—
Us'ns, us'ns, us'ns.
I'll say it— between you and me—
Worship how you want, who you want.
God or Satan.

Tall pine trees. And Indians,
Did I mention them?
Did I mention Indians?
Sewee and Witherbee, Echaw, Wambaw,
A touch of that red race shadowed in
Half the black, half the white faces,
Half the black white faces. Hellholian.
Ghost of red men and women stepping out of
Every crossroad's gas station.
There standing on every other
Halfway Creek deer stand
Holding Browning shotguns.
There on what they want to call
Center Line Highway,
'Cause the road runs
Half in Berkeley County, half
In Charleston.
Mother earth split by
Nothing more than paint dashes.
Sab Cumbee killed how many?
And Mr. McCay: he was robbed and
Shot dead at Palmer Bridges.
Mr. Charles Greenland McCay
Murdered on April Fool's Day
Eighteen hundred and seventy-nine.
Round up time, he had the money on him.
He'd sold those wild cows they'd
Driven cowboy style to town.
To Town.
He'd seen enough of town
And was anxious to get home.

Tobacco barn and sweet gum tree, Johnsonville, S.C.

Barn, chinaberry tree and pump, Nesmith, S.C.

MY LAST COMBINE

My last combine?

That's her in the red shed.

Sell?

Oh, no.

Another man might not take the time.

You with me?

The building is gone but Mr. McKenzie's cotton compress remains, Shirley, S.C.

Road through the living room, Oakridge Community, S.C.

BROTHER

The sky is low, the clouds are gray,
A single bird flies by
There a roof of rusted tin.
Beneath that silent sky.

And now a sudden wind complains
of how his day has been;
He hadn't meant to wait so long
And neither God had I.

See, I've come to sort my memories.
Just past the city's line
Unpainted clapboard siding,
With no occupants but mine.
And those are memory's people
The ones I left behind.

Daddy's there out in the yard.
That drink he needed bad.
Is this to be a happy drunk.
It's happy, mean, or sad.

The door is half-off its hinges
I push a passage wide.
There's Mama at her Singer,
I feel her treadle stride.

She is lighting with the oil lamp
Power's been knocked off.
With her feet and fingers flying.
She hums a tune that's soft.
And now bless me with your smile
My seamstress mother mild.

Oh, But Brother? Where is Brother?
Airport across the lane?
She nods. She hardly has to say
He's gone up in that plane.

So I am back out in the yard.
Sky has turned all blue.
From here to Halloween it's
Autumn blue straight through.

Daddy's on his feet
A palm to shade his eyes
'Cause here comes Brother
Dropping,
From way up in the sky.
And now he goes to turning.
A bird of orange dun.

He does a couple back flips
His daily battle's won.
Words can't do him justice
The world's just gone away.
My brother goes sky
Diving almost every day.

And now he's slipping sideways
Solemn ripping flight
He passes by the sun.
A bird of orange bright
Young Icarus grown bold
Then down he falls
And down he falls
He stuns my earth-bound soul

Gum ball, Cottageville, S.C.

It's a memory hard as Monday.
The chute a blossoms white,
He rocks upon light breezes
Then settles. Oh, the fights
He had with Daddy.
They are so far away.
Brother pulls a cord.
That says Don't you stay

And now the wind's turned cold.
Gray again, gray the sky,
Moaning, gray and lean and low.
I'm headed for the car.
Wondering why'd I come this far?
Except I know
That at this place
I was loved. That's something.
To be loved.
For like that spreading silk
Love does blossom
Love does grow.

Flock of cattle egrets touch down near an idle tractor, Pineville, S.C.

OH, YOU GODS

Oh, you gods and glorious Liberty
Bless these soybeans and the Land
And while you're at it, bless the Man
Who drives this big green tractor.
He's had about all he can stand
Of inclement weather and extraneous factors.

CROWS AND OTHERS

That crow I met here yesterday
Came back and brought a friend.
They asked of owls and corn fields
And carried on no end.

A beat of wing, an arch of white,
A call of kuk, kuk, kuch.
And now the egret's started in.
It's fish and crabs and such.

I had no answers for those three,
Least none they'd understand.
My take on the birds' broad world
Is from a narrow land.

Egrets at "Fish Cleaning Station," Eddytown, S.C.

Two ring-billed gulls vie for a perch, McClellanville, S.C.

OH

Oh, sweet despair.
We have arrived.
At the digital age.
As of this moment
Everybody knows
The price of this,
The life of him,
The start and end of everything.
Sure, gardens can still grow,
But there's no telling what
Comes up.
And love will find a way,
But there's no telling where.

Only two bream so far this morning, Lake Marion, Eutaw Springs, S.C.

Whelk shell pile, McClellanville, S.C.

Brown pelican enjoying the sun, Georgetown, S.C.

DO WE FEAR

Do we fear the mermaid's rocking chair
which rocked with great emotion
sets in motion
waves of grand proportion
and raises wild storms above?
Should we cringe at planetary notions
of star-crossed lovers
set adrift on luminous night seas
to churn and churn with monstrous oars
from monstrous oarlocks slipping free?
Churn so until the world is boiling?
Do we? You and I beneath these kinder skies?
We should and shall but not too much,
for what are we but comely piles of dust.
Cut off the light and say good night
to all but the bright implausible.

Shrimp boat, crab pots and pelicans, Edisto, S.C.

Jeremy Creek, McClellanville, S.C.

THE CAPTAIN'S SONG
There is a world where all things float
A world of light and crystal boats.
There is a world where trips don't end.
Where distant trawlers pass
With try nets pulled by laughing men,
Who know the Bay, the Keys, the Bell
Who've seen the sun rise all their life
And caught the barge hang once or twice.

If there's a hell
It'd be some Texas port,   ·
So far from home, on last report,
You couldn't run there
Not from here.
Not from Heaven whose bounds are clear.
Bull Shoals, Capers, maybe.
Running up to North Santee.

What you see?
          Nothing to it.
     Don't lie. Not in heaven.
          Nothing.
     You setting back on nothing?
          Clear shrimp. Two baskets.
          Maybe.
          Who can say
          Spilling 'cross the deck that way.
          Let me get some coffee.
     Just tell me 'bout the tow.
          Twenty baskets. A crab or two.

And so.
Just so you'll know.
On laughing men.
The ranges close
As they have closed before.

Preparations for Captain Jimmy Scott's funeral, McClellanville, S.C.

Clipped-corner door of Moseley Store, Lane, S.C.

A STUDY

I wonder will they slip away,
Go to where the plots of murder mysteries lay
Waiting 'til that last page when I say aloud,
Why, I've read this.
Or worse yet, drift out as far as
Where I put my glasses,
The tinted pair that make me
Look like . . . you know . . . you know he was
In *Five Easy Pieces* . . . like him
Now that his hair has thinned and his face is
Nothing but wide nose and sagging skin beneath which
The blood bumps along like clotting cream.
Him. You know the one I mean.
Is this hell? Forgetting where I put you. If so I pray
That all else goes away,
Travels to the moon where antique thoughts like swallows stay
And those I love remain so close it seems like yesterday.

Two latches, one lock, Macedonia, S.C.

Log construction, Earle, S.C.

How much longer can it stand? Pineville, S.C.

EASTER 2011
Tube Rose snuff was just
An ordinary part of life
And Nehi stained lips orange.
No one thought that strange.
Strange. That'd be Australia
With kangaroos, boomerangs
And living upside down.
Strange. Why the Communists
Have got a bomb
So monstrous big
It takes a fleet of trucks
To drag it through the streets.
Damnest thing we've ever seen,
Onion bulbs for roofs
And people there got no idea
Whatsoever of the truth.
Mister Nikita Krucheff,
Jesus Christ died for you.
Won't somebody help this man?
Teach him
Now I lay me down to sleep,
I pray the Lord my soul to keep.
Better yet, I pray I wake.
Before it is too late
Should I unwind the clock?
Granny's prickly Chinaberry tree
Seemed so high and wide
I never thought to climb another.
And even now I'm thinking
Likely when you reach the top
It's the same as any other.

Tar-papered barn, near Vance, S.C.

No more music, Wells, S.C.

If
If a volcano unsuspected
Erupted
And smothered us
Just as we are,
Done with supper
And watching a BBC mystery
On satellite TV
And happy,
Would it be so bad
Two thousand years hence
To have the pumice chipped away,
To be buffed and polished and
Placed on display
With some plaque
In a language of that later day saying:
Here is how they lived.
They didn't know what hit 'em?

Two-tone house, Cherry Hill, S.C.

Chairs on porch, near Carvers Bay, S.C.

Old-fashioned doorknob and lock, Cades, S.C.

DOING THE MATH

A naught is just ought
It's a dull aching pain
For the gold in a ring
I should've exchanged
One minus two
Alone is just one
I'm lonely,
I'm lonely,
I'm lonely plus some.

He's doing the math
While he's doing the town
You know love minus love
That's lost minus found
Love is for two
Alone is for one
I'm lonely
I'm lonely
I'm lonely plus some.

Adding, dividing.
I was keeping a count.
This day from some day
Hellacious amount
Love is for two
Alone for one
I'm lonely
I'm lonely
I'm lonely plus some.

A one dog manger
And a bird on the wing
Just six ways to Sunday
Do teach me to sing
I'll be your wife
You'll be the one
Be with you
Be with you
Be with you plus some.

The message door, Alcolu, S.C.

Lady Bankshire Rose and little log store, Jamestown, S.C.

OKAY
Praying to the God
Of simple things
Should be simple.
The trouble is
Where do you begin?
You there, hear our prayer.
That might do
But then it mighten',
And anyway, who's to say
He's listening?

Leaning log shed, Kingstree, S.C.

Nails were cheap, near Claussen, S.C.

Tobacco plants, Bowman, S.C.

Cotton plant, Hood Community, S.C.

Log construction, Trio, S.C.

A-framed chicken coop, Vance, S.C.

SUSIE'S POEM

Hope is a thing with feathers
Made with God's delight.
Here a comb, there a tail,
It sounds a call despite
The dark resolve of night,
To settle here with bleak despair,
Our feathered hope shouts, "Light!"
He tells us of a dawn,
Of a task, a joy, a fight.
It's time to be up and doing,
Gird your loins, quench your thirst,
Achieve, pursue, love full and well,
But feed the chickens first.

Outbuilding at "Old Hart Farm," Vance, S.C.

House and barn combo with fire hydrant, Gilbert Crossroads, S.C.

Farm animals, Tillman, Luray and Georgetown, S.C.

CHICKEN STEAK SONG
I've had my mama's corn bread muffins
And her mama's turkey stuffing
But Son that just ain't nothing
No. No. No. Make no mistake
When I look down at the plate
It's chicken-fried steak
I want to see.

I don't know how she'll do it.
Catch a chicken I suppose.
Then bring a cow and with some luck.
Cluck, cluck, cluck, cluck, cluck, cluck
She'll put the two together.
And add a little grease.
Collard greens you can keep 'em
And sweet potato pie.

You can have that R.C. Cola
I want a woman who can fry
Steak so it tastes like chicken.
Do not ask me why.
When I got my arm around her waist
And look down at that plate
I want to be a looking at
A golden chicken-fried steak.

Smoking chimney, Jamestown, S.C.

HELEN'S SONG
The pup had crossed the road.
Something dear there,
I suppose.
Here, she says.
Hey, hey. Here.
And here he comes.
Ears flying.
Tail adrift.
She smiles and says
You can't talk to a dog,
Not about important
Things. I've seen my
Husband do it,
Go on and on and on
Happy for an audience.
I only trust the chickens.
What's told there
Goes no further.
They know enough of life,
Of toil and pain and strife,
To understand
And tell no one.
A chicken keeps a secret.

Dirt road and power line leads to distant farm house, Cameron, S.C.

Emmy's Garden

My goodness. Look what you've done
That orange circle, that's the sun.
And this figure that's a man...
Oh. That's Adam.
Then all this squiggly hair,
That'd be Eve.
You took such care.
Just two outlines, still all there.
Ten digits each and bearing sin.
Thank you, God. You did your best.
We'll flesh in the rest.

Graveyard art, St. Stephen, S.C.

Daphne

Well, now, let's see.
Either through maleficence
Or in some dark devotion,
If a god should do it,
That is turn you into a tree,
If to keep a maiden pure,
Narrow leaves are woven
From your silky hair,
Your fingers become twigs,
For birds to perch upon,
While branches blend protesting arms,
If perfect whirls of bark are
Fashioned from your breasts,
If trunk from sloping belly grows,
What else may willful gods bestow?
If in metamorphosis,
Sweet moistness should be lost,
When swift legs and feet form
Roots that spread and tumble into earth,
If, and if, and if, and if...
A grave mischance,
But still perchance,
If this should happen,
And I do say if,
Remember me in spring time
'Cause I'll gladly make
believe. I'll bring a picnic basket
Spread a cloth upon the grass,
And we'll salvage what we can
Of your sweet equivalency.
But of course the same would go
If we find you aren't a tree.

Pitch Landing: In perspective

Each leaf that floats a golden boat
With mites on board to crew her
Each stump or leaning log
The promise of safe harbor.
But an otter turns and turns again
And sends great ripples raging.
The crew is to the rigging.
The leaf is breached.
No prayers can halt
And end complete
But then she rights
To sail away
Unsullied but contrite.
I saw it happen just this way
Or near enough in measure.
All hail these conquering heroes
And bless my own endeavors.

Rocking

I know Grandmama's rocking.
In that place up in the sky,
Where Aunt Rhoda's always waiting
For the Old Gray Goose to die.
For the goose to reach the mill pond,
And stand upon her head.
I've got that sleepy feeling
It's time to go to bed.

COMBAT

Timid.
He's sculpted so before the throw.
Afraid to close, our bronze hero
Stops to fling his javelin.
I know for
I approach the garden
In the same pose.
From a safe distance
And with eyes shut tight,
I toss the rake
Hoping through pure chance
To make an indention
In the ranks
Of the cauliflower
And carry off a head
Of lettuce,
In the process
Letting my wife,
Who watches from the safety of the kitchen,
Mistake cowardice for laziness
In dealing with the lettuces.

A POEM FOR DUFF

A man who hunts turkeys
Can do just one thing.
And that is hunt turkeys.
Oh, Dawn. Oh, Spring.

SANDPIPERS

Pipers come in sixteen brands
Each marked with colors of the sands.
Some grayish white, some whitish tan.
So I took the course to understand
Which bird was which, exploring
Close the tilt of rump, length of bill,
The rhythm of each probing.
But now in winter's hard embrace,
I see it's all but of a place.
The wave retreats and they descend,
To bend and peck and bend and peck and bend
Then, with wave's return, scurry up to higher sand,
Some grayish white, some whitish tan,
The sand that is.
The birds, that band
Of nondescripts,
We'll call a mottled crew.
But wait, wait, I don't belong...
Oh, Lord. In sympathy I've gone too far,
Stayed too long and with shoes on
Stand ankle deep
In their world of wonder.

Yard art, Santee Circle, S.C.

Wild Iris, Honey Hill, S.C.

BLUE IRIS

What a mongrel country.
Ripped, chipped
And stood on end to dry.
Not surprising then,
That one small swamp
Says it's done with men.
Says it clear, you come again
Blue flags will raise theirselves,
Flytraps will spread their mighty jaws
And this time
You will hear the roar.

THIS SEEMS TO WORK

The saddle on the sofa,
The reins behind the door.
A man is for a season.
A horse is evermore.

Tree and shadows frame view of cabin with rust-striped roof, Suttons, S.C.

Fire left only a chimney and a few block piers standing, Red's Landing near Andrews, S.C.

House in cotton field, Cameron, S.C.

FORT KNOX CAN'T HOLD A CANDLE

Fort Knox can't hold a candle
To these gold and silver years.
Why, the hair she's combing now,
It's shining silver white.
Yes, this is the richest bank
We sleep on every night.
A bank without the iron bars,
Secured without alarm,
There's gold in every sunset
This bank is just a farm.

Four small houses, Ridgeville, Tillman, Jamestown and Dorchester, S.C.

Waist-high broom straw surrounds little house, Jamestown, S.C.

Pecan tree arches over grand farm mansion, Holly Hill, S.C.

Weathered, two-story country store with addition, Workman, S.C.

SOME
Some had it
that dogs were the
last best hope
of man on earth
Cats said cats.
Don't listen.
Cats suffice
for catching mice,
But for somethun'
like last hopin'
Love is needed
And even adoration.

Man and his best friend, Workman, S.C.

Porch and rockers, Hampton Plantation

SANTEE 1937

I

Boiling clothes bright in a black iron pot
Smoke rising straight into November's blue rim.
It dare not follow her across the yard
Where white sheets hang, each trimmed
Upon a line which sags and rises,
Held in tension by gum poles so freshly cut
Their purple leaves, still unknowing, shimmer.
"Go child. Go from here. And let that chicken be."

Column cornice, Hampton Plantation

II
She did just fine.
The one-eyed doe,
She moved with care
A little slow,
Until a sun's eclipse
Crept into the light.
She turned her eye
Towards the sky.
Then for that short,
Uncertain space,
She ran
With all the soaring grace
God placed
Inside a deer.

III
The buck had found a short cut,
A way he thought
I would not go.
He crossed the further garden,
Took the narrow path,
Past The Pink Perfection, the one
My first wife planted. Delicate
And concise blooms. Twice
I've thought to cut a graft from there
But have not...
Could not.

View from under porch, Hampton Plantation

IV
In the moon shadow,
Why them with eyes may see.
Miss Anne. He think she be
The flower
That perfect one.
No, no, no.
That doe what run.
That Miss Anne.
"Child, get 'way,
Get 'way from that chicken."

200

A poet's home on the river, Hampton Plantation, near McClellanville, S.C.

Fogged-in ring-billed gull perches on bridge across the rediversion canal, Cross, S.C.

Cypress trees and their reflections, Russellville, S.C.

Wrought iron cross on cemetery gate, McClellanville, S.C.

VILLAGE CEMETERY

Of what substance is a sadness made
That thoughts unbidden there attend
Those of us who wait in dappled shade
Where graves, oaks and pines contend
In this our gentle village of undoing.

For love and acquisition
How brief is our pursuing.
How blessed common are the bounds
That God has placed us in.
Of all of this there is an end.
And then a new beginning.

MARSH

Listen to the marsh.
It stirs and pops and hisses.
The tide has slipped across the bar
And makes the night complicit.
Sweet brush of death,
An owl swoops low,
My hat to be his supper.
A warning that: to stand and go.
Who knows what stars might take me for,
Some beaten, broken shore,
A twisted stump of cedar,
A muddy creek where current scores
Out wrinkles brown and deep,
Yes. Time to rise, to slip away
Towards a promised sleep.
Sinew molded to the dark,
In triumph soft I hum.
Hear the peep and peep and peep.
Frogs, your hero comes.

Small bush grows from top of dock piling, McClellanville, S.C.

Workboats at rest, Jeremy Creek, McClellanville, S.C.

SONG FOR MINDY
Sing the body durable.
No prayer is enough,
No song too long.
As a child I drew
And drew.
Left no margins.
Don't say it.
Don't say "Put away the crayons."
I'm not done.
Not yet.

Cyclist and tree canopy . . . life and reflection, McClellanville, S.C.

Selden B. Hill is a photographer, pen and ink artist, historian, and the founding director of The Village Museum at McClellanville, S.C. In earlier years, he worked as a type setter and layout artist, played a lot of pool, and sold a lot of furniture, and in the opinion of his friends each occupation, in its own way, has helped to make him a better photographer. As museum director, he's offered encouragement and employment to both photographers and writers and curated many photography shows. Along with Susan Hoffer McMillan he is the author of the photography collection *McClellanville and the St. James Santee Parish* published in 2006. He still spends his free time exploring the less traveled paths of the South Carolina Lowcountry. Nothing gives him greater pleasure than stumbling upon the perfect photographic subject: a derelict tobacco barn framed by live oaks, with white puffy clouds overhead, and dark streaming shadows in the foreground.

A lifelong resident of the Carolina Lowcountry, *William P. Baldwin* is an award-winning novelist, poet, biographer and historian. He graduated from Clemson with a BA in History and an MA in English. He ran a shrimp boat for nine years then built houses, but the principle occupation of his life has been writing. His works include *Plantations of the Low Country*, *Low Country Plantations Today* (both with architectural photographer N. Jane Iseley), and the oral histories *Mrs. Whaley and her Charleston Garden* and *Heaven Is a Beautiful Place*. The screen play for the latter earned him a Silver Remy at this year's Houston Film Festival. For its depiction of Southern race relations, his novel *The Hard to Catch Mercy* won the Lillian Smith Award. Most recently he collaborated with photographer V. Elizabeth Turk on *Mantelpieces of the Old South* and supplied the text for chef Charlotte Jenkin's *Gullah Cuisine: By Land and by Sea*.

William P. Baldwin's list of books:

Plantations of the Low Country, text and picture captions with photographer Jane Iseley; *Charleston*, text and picture captions with photographer Jane Iseley; *Day Trips from Charleston: A Guide to the Carolina Low Country*; *Lowcountry Daytrips* (revised) with photographer Polly Walton des Francs; *Low Country Plantations Today*, text and picture captions with photographer Jane Iseley: Legacy Publications.

The Hard to Catch Mercy, novel; *The Fennel Family Papers*, novel; *Mrs. Whaley and Her Charleston Garden*, memoir; *Mrs. Whaley Entertains*, memoir: Algonquin Press.

A Gentleman in Charleston, novel; *Heaven Is a Beautiful Place*, memoir; *Journey of a Hope Merchant*, memoir: USC Press.

Mantelpieces of the Old South, photography collection, text and picture captions with Elizabeth Turk; *Inland Passages: Making a Low Country Life*, essays; *A Guide to the Iron Work of Charleston*, *Sacred Places of the Low Country*, *Plantations of South Carolina*, *Gracious Beaufort*, text and picture captions, photos HABS Photography collections; *William McCullough, Southern Painter, in Conversation with William Baldwin, Southern Writer*, oral history: History Press.

Charleston: My Picture Guide to a Holy City, essays and photographs: Village Museum.

Picturing the South: 1860 to the Present, photographers and writers, editor Ellen Dugan: Chronicle Books.

Gullah Cuisine: By Land and by Sea, cookbook with chef Charlotte Jenkins, photographs by Mic Smith, paintings by Jonathan Green: Evening Post Books Joggling Board Press.

His work has also appeared in *Garden and Gun*, *Charleston*, *Southern Living*, *Veranda*, *Victoria*, and *Southern Accents* magazines.